HEAVEN
IN YOUR
HANDBAG

Dear Lynette,

    I thought a missionary's daughter might appreciate this missionary's grand-daughter's offering.

        Peace and Blessings,

        Maxxi

           03-03-08

HEAVEN
IN YOUR
HANDBAG

A modern devotional
for women

Mazzi Binaisa

DARTON·LONGMAN + TODD

First published in 2006 by
Darton, Longman and Todd Ltd
1 Spencer Court
140–142 Wandsworth High Street
London SW18 4JJ

ISBN-10: 0-232-52689-3
ISBN-13: 978-0-232-52689-9

A catalogue record for this book is available
from the British Library.

Designed and produced by Sandie Boccacci
Set in 10/12pt Usherwood Book
Printed and bound in Great Britain by
CPI Bath

For the glory of God,
creator of heaven and earth and
all things seen and unseen.

And also for my late mother,
Princess Irene Marjorie Kabamoli Binaisa:
Thank you, Mummy, for showing me what
a woman of God looks like, feels like and
most importantly acts like.

CONTENTS

A PILGRIM'S PROGRESS

DEVOTIONALS – even those written by women with a penchant for procrastination, who are often accused of loquacity that borders on the compulsive and who can spend a whole day leafing through glossy magazines, grazing on gourmet morsels from the local delicatessen and sitting with friends talking about everything and nothing, or better yet trudging through record stores and buying vinyl (yes, there are some of us out there who are not entirely digitalised), or milling around all of Saturday in different accessory departments pondering bags and shoes – always, always, always need a prologue.

After all, there needs to be a premise, a 'why this' and 'why now' moment. I could start with the obvious, my total belief in God, in his person, made manifest in his son Jesus and the enduring power of the Holy Spirit. However, though that is true and I do completely and totally believe it, it wouldn't be a true reflection of how this devotional began and why I hope it will help, comfort and entertain those who choose to read it. As with all prologues, it is only fair that I set the scene.

I have often been told that my life story would read like a daytime soap opera were it not for the fact that it was true. State House at five (my father was President of Uganda), house arrest at six (the joys of being in Kwame Nkrumah's words a 'prison graduate'), escape out of Africa and into Hampshire boarding school at six-and-a-half and then an adolescence spent in London where the usual period of angst and agnosticism loomed large. In fact, I was large, lonely and pretty much ignored by the opposite sex and felt that if God really cared then he would make an appearance and change my circumstances or at the very least give me some clues as to how I could become more cool.

Oh, and how could I forget my mother – the original 'yummy mummy' – who successfully combined being godly, producing a netball team of children, running a household and businesses with alacrity, giving to charity anonymously (a fact we only found out when the recipients of her donations showed up at her funeral many years later), snapping back to a sample dress size with the birth of each child and having a game-over wardrobe and sense of style that managed to be unobtrusive and not detract from her core Christian characteristics and actions.

As an adolescent, both the remarkable and the unremarkable episodes and characters of my formative years were played out to the requisite soundtrack of boy-band crushes, numerous trips to wild fowl reserves (the ducks and geese were my homies in the absence of human ones) and a burgeoning obsession with cookery and fashion (better to drown the senses in tarragon chicken and pictures of the latest couture runway shows than be reminded that it's a Saturday night and everyone in your year, bar you, is attending the prefects' ball (the local boys' school's prom equivalent).

This is not to say that I hadn't been made aware of the power of prayer, or of God's omnipresence, or that I had tuned out God. In the above-mentioned soap, God had made a habit of turning up at the most opportune times. Going back to the house arrest period: it was whilst I was here languishing in a small house with my parents, our only occasional visitors my grandparents, that I learnt the Lord's Prayer. Every morning and evening I would say it out aloud and my favourite part was the last: 'for thine is the kingdom, for ever and ever', which, as I became better acquainted with my New Testament, I found was not part of earlier translations. In those words I was struck by the totality of God's sovereign power and the eternal nature of his character. For my simple faith it was enough that God controlled a kingdom that was bigger than the four walls in which we were incarcerated, bigger than a country, or a guard who was handy with an AK47. Furthermore, God's tenure was not contingent on any outside agency, and operated beyond time and space.

During this period, my late grandfather, Reverend Canon Ananias Juuko Binaisa, taught me that if you really believed, there was nothing that could over- whelm you and that God could and would intervene. So when we had our prayer marathons with my parents and grandparents, praying for a day when we would be free and see the other members of our family, I would silently add to my personal entreaties to God an extra please with chocolate and 7Up to drink for God too. (I *was* a child at the time and figured that as God had created chocolate and 7Up he must like them as much as me so it was only fair he was thanked accordingly!) When we escaped, unharmed, and I sat down to my first glass of 7Up in sunny Nairobi, I thanked God and placed the credit firmly at the foot of the cross.

However, like many a full-on Child-Christo, my faith depreciated with age. By the time I hit adolescence, I had replaced my simplistic but highly effective relationship with God with hostility towards him. In place of the calm and happy attitude I became a person riddled with doubts and fears. What made the situation even more insidious was the fact that I used my intellectual mind to construct an argument to justify and rationalise my negative thought processes. Let's also not forget that I was in sensory overload mode as depicted earlier, zoning out the feelings of loneliness that I felt rather than sharing them with a loved one or working through them with God.

By the time I hit my twenties I was flummoxed by the same questions that many people my age were also asking: Why wasn't I valued? Why the seemingly endless suffering? Why was everyone else so much more sorted compared to me? And will I live my life alone, or worse, stumbling from one awfully unfulfilling relationship to the next? To me it was not fair or right that good people should be first in the queue when misfortunes were being doled out. This is not to say that I stopped believing in God. I would describe it as if we were not – or rather *I* was not – on good speaking terms. I would pray to him in an ad hoc, part-timer kind of way, but concerted and careful applications were sadly absent.

However, external tragedies, most significantly my mother's first stroke and subsequent disabilities, the worst episodes occurring during my student days, got me back in church and a little more willing to be open to God's healing power. Or just plain desperate for his healing power. Church in itself was not a healing salve. I went through the same 'I-don't-know-anyone-this-is-flipping-awful' moments that had me hurtling back to my un-cool and un-cute teenage persona. However, it was cosy chats and discussions on the bible that were both intellectually rigorous and not couched in suspicion if you asked a challenging question, plus the added bonus that there was a fabulous patisserie (not in the church, that would have been too much) just down the road, that encouraged me to continue exploring the central tenets of my faith within the context of church attendance.

An improved relationship with God ensued. We became officially on full speaking terms again after I received him back into the heart of my life rather than in his previous place, at the periphery with an occasional star turn at the centre, usually when I was in a spot of bother. Placing God truly at the centre all of the time, rather than on an 'ad hoc as I feel' basis didn't stop me being me. Quite the opposite, I felt more at ease being my entirely random self, and being accepted for it, especially in light of the fact that it was God who had made me that way.

Furthermore, I discovered that a deeper relationship with God was like any other. You get to know one another (although he already knows you, but we'll get back to that one). He calls you to trust him, and you have your shocker-diva moments. Mine came when my impecunious state meant that frequent forays to Brompton Cross and other smart shopping emporia were out of the question and when two men in my life chose to be with women who in my estimation I was WAY better than (more on these later). But slowly as the fog of my own emotions began to clear it all started to make sense. And when it didn't there were all these fab tools that I had picked up from others further or deeper in their walk with God to use to help me get back on track

But getting back to the beginnings of this book, those aforementioned 'why' questions kept making frequent appearances, often at 'girlie sessions' with my friends over carb-rich food and good bottles of red, and increasingly the heart-warming platitudes that we were all very good at giving one another didn't work their expected magic. However, as I prayed answers began to emerge and I began to write them down. The actual content of this book started as an email ministry for my friends, some of whom have come to faith, others who are still asking questions, all of whom would send me emails charting the various news that was happening in their lives. Rather than write back a consoling, but ultimately not that helpful, email, I attempted to view the issue at hand in the light of biblical teaching and use answers based on what was emerging from my prayer time when I would ask God similar sorts of questions. My responses would always include a quote from the bible, along with a brief exposition that related to the problem and so my nickname, which has since stuck, of 'Pastor Mazzi', was born.

Before long these emails took on a life of their own as they were forwarded to others and I began receiving emails from people I didn't know with thoughts,

*'Be strong, all you people of the land,' declares the
LORD ... 'For I am with you.'*
Haggai 2:4

All of the biblical quotations within this book are from
the New International Version (NIV) translation. In
addition to God's word I have also learnt from and
been inspired by a number of Christian writers and
thinkers including: St Thomas Aquinas, St Augustine, St
Benedict, Charles Spurgeon, Fr John Wooley, Bishop T.
D. Jakes, Richard Foster, Phillip Yancey, John Ortberg
and Bruce Wilkinson. I have also been especially
encouraged by the following church leaders: Reverend
John Peters at St Mary's Bryanston Square, Pastors
Henry Biney and William Cancum at Trinity Baptist
Church and Prophetess Charlotte Ibrahim of The
Ministry of Jesus Christ.

Finally, I would like to thank my original 'pastorate'.
In alphabetical order (so no grumbling, girls!), Afua,
Anisa, Isobel, Jackie, Jay, Nina and Tamara. Also all of
my sisters in Christ at St Mary's Bryanston Square:
Aileen, Bimpe, Hannah, Josephine, Liz, Lorraine,
Rachael, Rehema and Rhonda, Last but not least, the
women with whom I share blood: Nakalema,
Naluwembe, Amooti, Michelle and Irene. May our
fruits go beyond our wombs and be seen in our works,
today and always.

MAZZI BINAISA
London 2006

YOU

A table set, just for two

It's all about you and him. No, not the beyond-cute guy who smells heavenly and has a smile that could melt a glacier. It's about you and God. He seems remote? Not quite in the same radius as you and El Cutie? Actually it has always been about you and him. He's known you for eternity. The measure of how well he knows you and how close this relationship is, is reflected in a psalm by David:

> *You know when I sit and when I rise:*
> *you perceive my thoughts from afar.*
> *You discern my going out and my lying down,*
> *you are familiar with all my ways.*
> **Psalm 139:2–3**

And, ladies, there's more:

> *Before a word is on my tongue*
> *you know it completely, O Lord.*
> **Psalm 139:4**

Pretty intense for a God who's remote. Removed. Detached. The thing is, we are never by ourselves. We are always in omniscient, omnipotent company. He is aware of all our comings and goings, eager to assist us and encourage us. He's the ultimate travelling companion for the journey of life and he won't elbow you out of the way to get to the window seat.

So how does one communicate with him? Back to the innocuous beginnings that led to the content of this book. My first forays into getting into the 'God zone' included concerted study of my bible and reacquainting myself with using a concordance, last seen in my 'A' level Religious Studies days, as well as magnifying his name through dancing, which I love, singing, which I do badly, and writing poetry, where I have a mixed success rate. Initially, I would get bogged down by the lack of tangible experiences I had with God. Sadly for me, I would reflect there was no burning bush moment in the middle of the shopping mall on a Saturday morning as a result of my spiritual efforts. Eventually I accepted that communicating with God is more often than not a metaphysical process.

Unfortunately, we can't go out for a fatter than fat dinner with God, pour out our heart, cry, rail, laugh and be in receipt of the Holy Spirit by the time the pudding course comes along. However, we can pray and this spiritual dialogue is the principal mechanism we have for connecting with our maker. Prayer styles and techniques have come in and out of fashion over the centuries rather like skirt lengths. One era it's all about smells and bells with incense and chimes a-go-go, in a church that has museum-standard altar pieces, ornate rood screens and real stained glass. Another century or two later it's praying silently on your knees. Still later, others opt for a chap in rocking raiment leading everyone in some call and response. Then it will be all about the congregation's participation, with people being led by the Holy Spirit to shout out their own prayers to God, whilst the pastor places a few well-cued 'Amens' and 'Hallelujahs'. But whilst it's interesting to note changes and rewarding to participate in the different styles, praying, rather like fashion, is often best done in a simple timeless way.

Whether we belong to an established supplication tradition (funky way of saying 'organised religion') or not, we all benefit from prayer as it is an opportunity for us to connect with and nourish the interior of our being. Most of us are well versed enough in regard to health to know that whatever we eat has a direct knock-on effect on our weight, energy levels and the success of our fitness levels or regimes. The same is true of our spiritual condition or what medieval writers called 'the inner man'. It is only when this is healthy and well fed that we can manifest a character or nature that reflects the best we can be.

> *'But when you pray, go into your room, close the door and pray to your Father, who is unseen. Then your Father, who sees what is done in secret, will reward you.'*
> **Matthew 6:6**

In this verse from Matthew, which is part of a lengthier exposition on prayer (See **Matthew 6:5–14** for the full picture), Jesus touches on the principle of the type of relationship that God wants from us in our prayer life. First of all he suggests that we go into a room, in solitude. This is so that there are no distractions of noise or of people. Not long ago, I attended a friend's church's Easter service and was reminded that church is not always the ideal place for quiet prayer. There were just too many gorgeous men in the congregation, my eyes were wandering all over the place and as a result the quality of my prayers suffered. With the exception of one from-the-heart exaltation to the Lord for the wonders of his male creation, I decided that in future I would only attend their socials! But on a serious note, the objective of prayer is to connect to God, our father in heaven, who is unseen. Most of our interaction in life involves using the five senses. We see paintings, listen to music, hold loved ones, taste food, smell flowers. Yet in prayer, we are called to go beyond the confines of our everyday human senses. For this demanding task it is important that the quiet place is found.

The second portion of the verse talks about secrecy. Again, this might seem a little random. People often ask their friends to pray for them, we share our inner-most trials and tribulations with others, so why should we keep our prayer life secret? Well, two reasons. First, prayer is not for show, it is not so that we can tell other people how 'hardcore holy' we are, that we are world champions of prayer. It is about connecting to God and to the spirit that resides in all of us that is a reflection of him. Prayer is about you and God together, conversing, sharing, celebrating and commiserating. Second, we will never be 100% honest in our prayer life if we feel we have to recount every in and out of it to another person. We *all* have filters, and even when we talk to those closest to us, there are things we hold back on. However, you are called to not hold back on God as he created you and calls you to trust him. What's more, once you have reached this intimate place with him, God can begin to bless every area of your life – quite an exciting prospect. So when you get a chance, get out the Diptyque candles, switch off the phone and have a chat with the person who knows the answers to *all* the questions you ever have asked, want to ask and will ask.

A former malcontent responds

If what I have just written seems a little trite, doesn't quite assuage your frustrations and makes you feel angry, I understand. Disappointment, despondency and on a deeper level despair are hard to reconcile. Sometimes, it seems too difficult to pray, too painful to talk to God, to see him as a friend and an active party in our life. It feels like nothing ever changes anyway, but I have a challenge to those in that particular space. To get beyond it, we need to start by banishing from our hearts anything that blocks our souls from singing freely, from our thoughts limiting our achievements, from nagging fears blocking the abundant and beautiful harvest that lies within all of us.

> But the fruit of the Spirit is love, joy, peace, patience, kindness, goodness, faithfulness, gentleness and self-control.
> **Galatians 5:22–23**

The Spirit that dwells within us is capable of reaping this harvest. What blocks us are the very things that are not of God, the polar opposites of the spiritual fruits listed in Galatians. This shopping list of the negative characteristics: impatience, meanness, evil, unfaithfulness, abrasiveness and indiscipline – it sounds more like a recipe for a disastrous existence than an effective way of being. Is it really possible to have love abundantly flowing in our lives, if we hold onto hatred? Who can truly say that they want to be happy if they are content in their own misery? How can we get the internal peace that all of us crave if we are at war with our selves?

What often holds us back is the mistaken notion that freedom and unbridled behaviour is the same thing. That the alternative makes for a monochrome existence. Nowadays, much is often said of the restrictiveness of living a God-centred existence. But what could be more restrictive than a self-centred existence? One where we cater only to our needs, care little for the consequences that our actions might have for others, respond in an 'only when it suits me' manner. It may sound tempting, but after a while we become our own jailers. For all of our moods and activities are predicated by us. Every time that we are depressed, angry or frustrated, if we rely solely on ourselves and never look to any outside agency for assistance, then we are stuck. Whilst exotic holidays, reclining in Eames chairs and sharing our feelings with others, medication and the like can alter our mood states, they never actually solve the underlying problem. It is for this reason that living only for ourselves can ultimately cause us pain, as a free-for-all in attitudes leads to our own destruction.

The second obstacle that can block us from the breakthrough God wants for us is our own hearts, which are calloused by circumstances. We turn over ideas formulated in words to prop up our ideologies and we stick rigidly to them, as even if they do not offer comfort at least they are an explanation and a formula for us to live by.

> *'What goes into a man's mouth does not make him "unclean", but what comes out of his mouth, that is what makes him "unclean".'*
> **Matthew 15:11**

In this verse Jesus illustrates exactly why words are so important. He is referring to dietary laws in this instance, stating that the purity of our heart is not contingent on keeping external rules, but rather the state of our heart is entirely dependent on what we feed it. It's not the chocolate éclair that makes the difference. It's the words that start out as thoughts which dwell inside us that cause the most damage. The whole personal development industry is built on the mantra of negative thoughts breeding negative results and this verse gives us a vivid picture of a heart, our hearts that are in desperate need of God's healing. However, there is further encouragement for those who choose to place their faith in God:

> *And hope does not disappoint us, because God has poured out his love into our hearts by the Holy Spirit, whom he has given us.*
> **Romans 5:5**

Once we allow this reality to seep through, a new relationship can be built. We can no longer accept the former distortions as being the sum total of our lot. Instead we have Divine hope and love that has been poured into our hearts that we might be renewed once more.

Strengthen that sinew

Though the fig-tree does not bud and there are no grapes on the vines, though the olive crop fails and the fields produce no food, though there are no sheep in the pen and no cattle in the stalls, yet I will rejoice in the LORD, I will be joyful in God my Saviour.
Habakkuk 3:17–18

I read those words and was shocked. Not at the content, but because they echoed a sentiment I knew only too well.

The Lonely Walk
Although the road is empty and the trees are
    stark
And morning and evening are one as it is so
    dark
Although the phone never rings and the house is
    not filled with laughter
I know you are with me
Sitting patiently, nudging indulgently, coercing
    gently
You are with me
You were there before you'll be there beyond
    and in between
Your power is intangible, untransferable, beyond
    logical
You are in me I am in you
You are my God
JMK 2001

Written in Hyde Park on a windy winter morning, 'The Lonely Walk' was a poem I wrote to convey the emotional place I was in. Cold, comparatively broke, feeling lost compared to my so-sorted friends, but still aware that somewhere, somehow God was in it. Walking with God can feel lonely. In those silent times, where it seems as if requests and entreaties to our creator and saviour are being ignored, when the promised harvest seems thin on the ground or worse, non-existent. The words 'Where are you?!!!' can easily ring through your ears. However, despite all of this, Habakkuk chooses to walk with him, just as I did. The other truth echoed in Habakkuk and to a humbler extent in 'The Lonely Walk' is that the self and God stay in communion and close companionship even in less than fantastic scenarios. Sometimes, it's just not working. Be it the footwear, the career, the relationship. But one relationship that never dies and is a constant is that with God. He is always there, even if our flesh-led, empirical, desiring eyes fail to see it.

There have been days that have been really hard. As I write this I am not working for a measurable wage. But God is working in me, constantly protecting and silently blessing me even when I forget to be truly thankful for his provision. Furthermore, Habakkuk calls us to 'be joyful in God [our] Saviour'. You see, the down times are not times of inactivity. It is in the struggle that we become more like him: incredible beings capable of victory through all manner of trials. Not only that, there is the assurance that God is cheering us throughout these trials.

There is an old-school English saying 'strengthen your sinew and gird your loins', the gird your loins bit coming directly from biblical references (Elijah called us to do it) and the strengthen the sinew, well let's just say that in the suffering in true stiff upper lip styles and fashions you're meant to toughen up. This sort of stuff might seem like the worst instance of cold-hearted platitudes, but there is truth in the importance of not allowing troubles to defeat you. The secular world talks of 'no pain no gain' and yet we often think that once we have accepted God into our lives the rest will be easy, that we will be in an extended love-in with our Lord and Saviour. Yet, just like the bizarre diet pill advertisements that promise instant size 8-dom results this would be false.

> *And the God of all grace, who called you to his eternal glory in Christ, after you have suffered a little while, will himself restore you and make you strong, firm and steadfast.*
>
> **1 Peter 5:10**

Our relationship with God is like any other. It will take us places, challenge us often and not necessarily lead us to neat chocolate-box conclusions. What brings us hope, however, is revealed in the above verse. Peter states that God himself will restore us. Our restoration is so personally important to him that he does not dispatch one of his heavenly hosts or angels to the scene of our hurt and anguish, but he personally and lovingly tends to our wounds, ensuring that we are in an even better state than we were previously. It is in these times, when God directly intervenes in the midst of our suffering, that we are offered the unique chance to engage in an intimate interaction with him. Faith-defining moments often happen in the midst of tribulation. It is easy to believe in a God who has our best interests at heart when things are good, it is a much greater challenge to trust him when things go awry. Perhaps, the suffering that we endure is not merely a question of building spiritual muscle but also offers us an opportunity to have an encounter with God to see the goodness of his heart and the grace and support he is so desperate to share with us all.

Self-spring clean and the new collections

Drawing nearer to God and aligning ourselves to his purposes will often result in an emotional transformation. The clear out can be extensive, but is absolutely essential.

> *Get rid of all bitterness, rage and anger, brawling and slander, along with every form of malice. Be kind and compassionate to one another, forgiving each other, just as in Christ God forgave you.*
> **Ephesians 4:31–32**

Turning our selves over to God is a spring clean of sorts. We have to discard our old and disturbingly comfortable emotions. After all, they have only been of limited success, and the fact that our souls still often ache is an indication of the need for God to truly enter our lives.

Allow me to expand: I have been fortunate to only have one affair of the heart that combusted on such a spectacular scale that I did not speak to the person for some time and vowed that I never would. At the heart of my pain was the fact that I had got it wrong about where our relationship was heading. I was certain, absolutely rock-solid sure, could have bet everything I had and coerced several others to have a flutter, such was my confidence that I would spend the rest of my days signing cheques of varying amounts with his surname as the reassuring suffix to my first name. (A double-barrelled surname combining my own surname and his was out of the question – it would have sounded ridiculous.)

The rationale that anchored this belief was lengthy. We had known one another for ages, had similar sorts of backgrounds, an almost identical aesthetic sensibility from food to literature, oh, and the rather more obvious he was just *too* handsome and smelled like my own personal notion of heaven. Of course there were difficulties and issues, but I thought that there was enough 'there', in terms of our relationship to last the long haul. After all, I reasoned, where was he going to find another replica of me, me the girl who in his own words, fit so many of his requirements? So I chilled, albeit in an extended emotional limbo of sorts, for although we were super intimate, there was never an 'It's official! Let's send our friends and family save-a-date cards and start finding out the costs of group bookings on flights to Africa' moment. He reasoned that we still had so much to do in cementing our respective careers, and that we both needed to be settled to have the best possible start.

However, things didn't work out that way. Put simply, he chose to settle down with someone else. What was worse for me was that the girl I 'lost-out to' was someone who was so different from me as to be my polar opposite. To say that I was shell-shocked would be an understatement. I railed at God. How could he have led me so fantastically up the garden path? This was *my man*! She couldn't even begin to understand him. They couldn't possibly have more fun together than we had. In the fall-out it was not only God that I railed at, but also Mr Never-Gonna-Be, and the result was that not only did we not remain friends, relations were *so* frosty between us as to be Siberian.

It was only when I decided after some time to begin to pray about finding love again that I realised there was something blocking me. Despite there being plenty of perfectly lovely candidates, I was blocked and hindered by my past pain. I had decided with the same vigour that I had once planned my future as being with Mr Never-Gonna-Be that there would never be another man that I would love in such an unconditional way. Furthermore, I was convinced that all of the relationships I had would result in my, after a lengthy trial period, being deemed to be not quite good enough. It was all too unbearable, and very slowly I began to grow bitter, angry and resentful about the fact that that particular part of my life was now effectively over. It was at this point that I realised the power and the relevance of Ephesians 4:31–32. It didn't matter how foxy the dress I was rocking or how perfectly my hair had been styled, I was still filled with bitterness and rage about the way my former relationship had ended. Bitter that I had been rejected, furious that God had let it happen. What was worse, I was filled with malevolent thoughts about the world at large. After all, what else could explain away my wilful disregard for the overtures of other men, who were merely expressing an interest?

My prayers and sharing my pain in fellowship led

me to embark on a process. Rather than be bitter that I was not with the one I thought I should be with, I thanked God for the time we had had together and for ending a relationship that may not have run a fruitful course. I put my rage towards God to one side and instead allowed him to enter the depths of my being where I needed healing from the rejection, and acceptance and reassurance for being the woman that he had painstakingly made and nurtured thus far. Obeying the slander part of the verse meant that I had to curb the urge to drink several double vodka tonics, become suitably melancholic and slate his decision to end our relationship to anyone who had the misfortune to be in my company. As to the malice, let's just say negative affirmations along the lines of 'Please let her decide that she wants to move to Outer Mongolia and herd sheep on her own rather than be with him' had to stop.

It was a process. After all, it is so much easier to live with the usual behaviours than overhaul them. But the longer I practised this doggedly, even when I didn't particularly believe that anything was happening, the more things did indeed start to change. For a start, I stopped waking up each morning with a pang in my heart. The feeling of being emotionally thwarted also started to subside. What was more I began to truly appreciate what was around me. The God I served was wondrous and what was more, if I really had accepted him as being not only omnipotent but also omniscient then surely there would be a plethora of examples of his magnificent creation?

I would love to conclude this brief testimony with a neat epilogue along the lines of the author is now living in a beautiful townhouse in Belgravia and villa in Africa with her God-fearing, intelligent, handsome and ludicrously sexy husband and their three chubby, friendly and polite children. However, that is not the case. Nevertheless, what I am aware of is that it is only in the altering of my mindset and the forgiveness of my former beloved that I can possibly get to a place of renewal and resolution. Furthermore, if I couldn't begin to forgive myself for getting it wrong, and him for hurting me, how could I really claim to want to follow God's precepts? It is in forgiveness that we are released from pain, as we are saying not so much that it did not happen, but that we do not wish to hold onto it. Rather like last season's Balenciaga that went with all of our old outfits, we are seeking an altogether new look, in keeping with our new Christ-like selves.

It is interesting to note how in many transformations or demarcation of God's favour in the bible a change in clothing is used symbolically. The prodigal son (for the full story see **Luke 15:11–32**), when he returns home penitent in his rags having squandered his inheritance and lived a life of penury and proclaiming himself to 'no longer [be] worthy to be called your son', is immediately given a new robe to wear, a ring with which to adorn himself, and some smart sandals to complete his look. This was not only an earthly makeover but a spiritual one. The prodigal did not belong to his old life any more, to the dysfunctional ways of operating that had seemed attractive but ultimately led to his financial demise. He was back in the bosom of his father, who not only was delighted to see him, but also went so far as to put on a spread of the most extravagant proportions for him. The parable is an allegory for the relationship that God desires to have with us. What blocks us from this new relationship are the old habits, the negative ways of thinking that block our true selves from stepping forth and leading a life under God's stewardship. It is for this reason that we are explicitly called to get rid of them. Just like a seasonal must-have that was so of-the-moment but now sits embarrassingly in the corner of the wardrobe never to be worn again, we must get rid of them, admitting that yes, we were wrong, and they never really suited us anyway. The new behaviours and attitudes will be just like the robes worn by the prodigal. God already has all of our measurements, some beautiful beyond-couture-quality pieces are waiting for us to wear, and an enormous party will be put on in our honour, as we are already promised:

> 'I tell you that in the same way there will be more rejoicing in heaven over one sinner who repents than over ninety-nine righteous persons who do not need to repent.'
> **Luke 15:7**

The notion of a sinner, or of being one, can discourage us from allowing our selves to connect with God. We can all probably recall an incident where we ourselves or someone we know has felt condemned and beyond reproach because of a person in a pulpit offering a lengthy exposition about everyone being on the fast track to hell. Yet this is an overly simplistic presentation of sin and being a sinner. We are all sinners because we all make mistakes, hurt others or choose to participate in things that we know are not productive or positive. The good news is that God loves us anyway and is seeking to restore us to the benevolent plans he had for us. Connecting with God is not a series of exams that we have to take, with the whole world watching and witnessing all of our errors. The same 'Purity Posse' that are proclaiming fire and brimstone on others, must themselves go through the same renewal process, and also slip up by virtue of their humanity. God loves all sinners whether they choose to allow him into their lives or not. What he is really interested in are our intentions and desires. If we desire him in our lives, if we look to improve our behaviour and conduct and if we are genuinely seeking change, there will be much rejoicing on his part. There should also be much rejoicing on our part too as we have actively taken a step into a new way of being. We have chosen to depart from the considered norms of low-level depression, covetousness and general emotional decrepitude and enter into a way of being where our heart, soul and very essence of our being finally receives the nourishment it so richly deserves.

LOVE

What's occurring?

Going home to Uganda has many benefits. First of all there is the sunshine and the pleasant breeze we experience by virtue of being at a high altitude but still on the equator. Then there are the verdant hills of Kampala, so lush as to look not so much painted, but Photoshopped to within an inch of their lives. Let us not forget the mango and avocado trees in the garden that provide breakfast and quick face-masks all in one go. And of course there are the relatives, mainly older, always loving, but with *one* pertinent question that they continue to revisit, in spite of it causing a perfectly pleasant family get-together to cloud over.

'Why are you not married?' asks the infamous 'friend of the family'.

'What's wrong with our daughter?' responds the aunt who has been itching to wear the hat with the ostrich plumes that she bought in the January sales 'just-in-case'.

'We'd better pray for her, but first I think we need to ask you why are you so picky?!' cries the recently-married cousin who has always been slightly suspicious of the level of effort you put into your love life in lieu of your career.

'Actually, my sister's son is in town. He is also looking. Although he was wanting someone, you know,

a little younger. After all … children and so on … '
interjects infamous 'friend of the family', who started
the conversation in the first place and is now finishing
it with a doom-and-gloom prediction because you are
no longer twenty-two and able, or particularly inclined,
to produce a football team for the likely lad.

There was a time when I used to involve myself in
the debate, defending the status of the single and
clamouring for a better deal or attitude from the elders
who brought it up. The level and the tone of loved
ones' enquiries into our love lives can often strike a
raw nerve. I have yet to meet a single woman who has
not at one point or another pondered her marital
status – her reaction of course being entirely dependent on whether she saw the be-all and end-all as being
a 'Mrs', or whether she found others' keenness
anachronistic and distasteful as she was still having so
much fun on her own. But for family, friends and the
random extras we know who see themselves as professional wedding attendees, the increasingly late
stage that we choose to settle down can cause concern. Yet it is when their concern transfers to us by
some strange emotional osmosis, making us anxious,
that we have true cause for concern:

> And we know that in all things God works for the
> good of those who love him, who have been called
> according to his purpose.
>
> **Romans 8:28**

This verse helped me get the rellies off my case and
to understand the whole love question in relation to
God. What was paramount was my love for God and
his infinite reciprocation of it. There was a benevolent

plan because the God I loved was a benevolent God. Instead of choosing to focus on my position of lack (as my relatives were doing due to the paucity of infants for them to spoil and lack of a groom to physically and intellectually dissect), I could instead focus on the fact that God works in every situation, including boyfriend-light and husband-absent ones. Also the final part of this verse talks about our 'calling to his purpose'. Sometimes, there are necessary processes we need to go through on our own to make us even half-way pleasing to another person on a long-term or permanent basis. We have spoken of this in the 'You' section of the book, when we talk of the journey into our soul that needs to be made for us to be a true reflection of the incredible women that God made us. But in this verse the notion of his purposes reminds us that ultimately everything we do in our lives is in the light of God who created us. His purposes and his calling are what are of paramount importance, rather than our own ideas of where we should be and what we should be doing.

It might seem like the 'perfect time' to be getting married, or 'Auntie' may have found a florist willing to offer tuberose on special in winter months for the church decorations, or your cousin may have sourced on the internet a fantastic wine wholesaler with a deal on non-vintage champagne, but if it is not serving God's purposes then it won't happen. What we must remember in all of the activity, virtual or otherwise by ourselves and others, is that his divine purposes are served in all of our conditions. Instead of focusing on the apparent current lack, the future 'what-ifs' and the past 'if-onlys' we should remind ourselves that everything that is happening to us is for his purposes and our ultimate good.

The boy-buffet

One of the things that living in this age appears to offer, particularly if you live in a town or a city, is the seemingly endless choice. Observe the rise and rise of convenience and snack foods. We've gone from a nation of three square meals a day to grazers or skippers of meals. Ask yourself how many people you know who actually sit down to three meals, two of which are warm? There just doesn't seem to be suffi- cient time or inclination to do such a thing. After all, why bother to cook if you're just cooking for one? Or what about all the other things that we don't have the time to do if we spend inordinate amounts of time peeling, sautéing or roasting? Isn't it easier to grab something on the hoof, and head off to the next appointment or event? After all, it's only food? Yet, this slap-dash attitude whilst working in the short term, as we are nominally 'sustained', often plays havoc with our health at a later date.

When I proposed to a friend of mine that perhaps we had the same attitude to our love lives she looked at me as if I had finally taken leave of my senses. But allow me to elaborate. You feel a hunger. Rather than pausing and actually figuring what it is you want to eat, you just grab the nearest and easiest thing and then, after you've taken a bite of it, you either discard it because it wasn't quite what you wanted or you com- plain bitterly and send a group email to everyone you know to boycott the dodgy takeaway where you ended up with a spot of food poisoning having opted for a 'quick bite'. And one could go on at length about 'canapé bulge' – a weight-gaining condition that occurs from living on the snacks proffered at drinks parties and smart soirees, when the large amount of delicious and delectable looking morsels results in a mini 'feastathon'.

The same patterns can be witnessed in our behaviour with men. It is so easy, in the fit of emotional hunger or loneliness, to 'sample' the first or easiest guy that comes along. After all, everyone else we know is doing it and modern society is based on the premise of 'quick fixes' being available for absolutely everything: we are told that we will have to 'kiss a lot of frogs before you find your prince' and that to 'try before you buy' is the only way we will know *for sure*. Yet it is this buffet dining approach to our relationships that makes us feel queasy, used, dissatisfied and, in the worst instances, sullied. Furthermore, if we really have accepted the notion of a God who actually has a plan, and a good one at that, then surely scoffing down the butterfly prawn, the mini lamb kebab or the chicken hot wings will not make us feel any better.

> *They think it strange that you do not plunge into the same flood of dissipation, and they heap abuse on you.*
> **1 Peter 4:4**

Written as part of a lengthier exposition of God-centred living (check out **1 Peter 4:1–11** for the full picture) and preceding a harsh rebuke of the former idolatrous living of the letter's recipients, Peter highlights the rough ride that is in store for all those who choose to overtly trust in God and not participate in their previous lifestyle. As you stand by the boy-buffet (whether it be in a bar, party, club or pub) and don't take a manic smash and grab approach to assuage those pangs of loneliness, the rest of the 'real world' will think you're nuts for not joining in. But the clue is in the choice of word of Peter in this verse for what the rest of the world is doing: 'dissipation'. Dissipation implies waste, and to call it a flood of waste, as Peter does, invokes a vivid image of wanton squander. We must try to remember that we are precious. God would not have made us in his image otherwise and Jesus would not have died for us if this were not the case. It is for this reason that we should attempt to refrain from participating in the manic melee for guys that is going on around us. I am not advocating a 'sit and wait for your dance card to be filled' approach. After all we have moved on from the era of the dance card, where girls would sit against a wall waiting for guys to fill their card requesting a dance (potentially nightmare-inducing if you're the unlucky girl with a dance card that is not even half full or even the girl with the one which is so full that it runs to two pages and your feet beg for mercy!). But we should pause and test what it is that we really want or more importantly need, and whether it is something that will enhance our walk with God or distract us or draw us away from it. The bible talks at length about 'discernment' and 'testing', and there is a lot to be said for assessing our choices of partner in a similar way.

> ... *preserve sound judgment and discernment, do not let them out of your sight ...*
> **Proverbs 3:21**

Utilising our spiritual eye more and our physical eye a little less will often result in more balanced choices and less catastrophic conclusions. In this lengthier passage about wisdom from **Proverbs 3 and 4** we are shown how the person who exercises discernment stumbles less, is covered by grace, and confident in the choice they make. For them there is no vacillation at the hors d'oeuvres platter. They know what is right for them, or at least have a better understanding of what is needed. Wisdom and discernment require patience as the answers are not always revealed in the time frame we seek. Going back to our food analogy, if we pause and consider what it is we need to eat, decide to take time in the preparation of the meal, and increase our understanding of the kind of nutrients we need, the choices become closer aligned to what God wants for us. In practical terms for us all it means less of the buffet-bites and more of the wholly nutritious, balanced and scrumptious suppers.

To 'step forward' or not?

'The thing is, I'm scared of looking like a complete joker because I love him so much.'

A group of us were staying in, having decided that loud bass bins and smoked-out hair were not the order of the day that particular Friday evening. My friend who was holding the floor was on her second (or perhaps third) glass of Argentinian Malbec. In that one sentence she had summed up a fundamental block in many relationships. The sheer terror of exposure, of letting our self-preserving guard down. Yet let us consider whether that same self-preserving guard could also become a self-embalming tomb. One where our true self lies trapped, unable to express, and in return experience and receive, the many facets of love.

There is much written within the pages of the bible, by philosophers, mystics, novelists and musicians about the multifarious nature of love. But at the centre of love gone awry between people is the feeling that the love they offer might not be enough. In his entreaty to the early church St John calls people to love one another by presenting a statement on what love is not.

> *There is no fear in love. But perfect love drives out fear, because fear has to do with punishment. The one who fears is not made perfect in love.*
>
> **1 John 4:18**

This verse needs to be contemplated upon with a verse that comes earlier in the same passage.

> *God is love. Whoever lives in love lives in God, and God in him.*
>
> **1 John 4:16**

The confidence to love and be loved can always be enhanced in a complete surrender to the Divine who *is* love. God's love for us is unconditional; its character is entirely selfless. But in this verse we are reminded that God's love, by virtue of being part of us, can also be expressed by us. Whilst long-stem roses, flawless diamonds and double-digit ply cashmere can most definitely enhance momentarily the outward expression of love, they do not add to the inward quality. If we accept this notion it becomes a shade easier to reject the fear of ridicule and leap gladly into exploring and delving into the depths of God's and others' love.

St John also talks about fear and its relation to punishment. Many of us have experienced the pain of being punished by those who professed to love us. It is so easy to get into the mind space of falling short. It might be that a loved one practised affection conditionally. The love you received being contingent upon getting the right grades for a parent, impressing a group of strangers in a room for friends, or fitting into a certain sized skirt for your man. The apostle says it all though, when he says that perfect love, the love of God, drives out fear. It sees fear for what it truly is, an unwanted interloper who has no business squatting in and generally trashing anyone's spirit. In that last sentence, 'The one who fears is not made perfect in love', St John places the ball firmly in our court. Challenging us with the statement that holding onto fear means we miss out on love.

So getting back to the original quandary posed by my friend and many like her, she needs to first put the glass of Malbec down for a couple of minutes, splash water on her face if it's necessary to do an express sober-up, and actively choose to have love in her life. It starts with accepting God's love, for loving you just as you are. We need to try to absorb the profundity of this reality. God's love really is unconditional. No catches, no small print, no government health warnings. An omnipotent God, a God who by definition does not need our love for he is love realised in his grace, personified in his Son and transposed on all by his Spirit. When God's love is fully accepted by us, we get the chance to feel the tangible difference of knowing that he dwells in us. And with that transformation comes alteration in our behaviour. Just as fear, which dwelt on uncurtailed, suffocated dreams, bred lassitude and dulled the soul, so God's love, dwelling within us, will breed hope, joy and optimism. It's really as simple a choice as that. God's love doesn't always mean that we get our own way. What it does give us is a confidence to share our heart, as it is a mere fraction of the affection and care that he has for us. Looking like a joker, as my friend had dreaded, is not so challenging or nerve racking. I mean, how can Divine love as it is reflected through us and then directed to a lucky guy, seem so bad? Or put mundanely, it can't be too hard to say you love someone when you have God's love as the ultimate back-up, pick-me-up and lift-up!

However, love is not meant to be an end in itself, especially when directed to another person. We are called into communion, into sharing our lives with someone else. Many of the people I know still hold the idea of meeting a life partner as their greatest desire. Yes, we may have the vote, be allowed to attend any higher learning institution, have equal inheritance rights and so on. Nevertheless, I have yet to meet an unmarried woman whose eyes do not glaze over to a greater or lesser degree at the thought of being proposed to, her perfect wedding day, or lying recumbent in an idyllic part of the world after said nuptials with a man who makes her stomach somersault at regular intervals. God saw the limits of creation as if it was just a world inhabited with men when he said:

> 'It is not good for the man to be alone. I will make a helper suitable for him.'
> **Genesis 2:18**

However, what happens after this passage is even more interesting. After God takes a rib out of Adam (ouch!) and makes a woman, Adam describes woman as this:

> *'This is now bone of my bones and flesh of my flesh ...'*
> **Genesis 2:23**

And still there is more, as God sets up the premise for relationships of the heart:

> *For this reason a man will leave his father and mother and be united to his wife, and they will become one flesh ...*
> **Genesis 2:24**

A feminist reading of this passage doesn't inspire. We could say it places woman as being described as subordinate, as she is described as a 'helper'. Woman is contingent as she was made out of just one rib. Furthermore, woman is trapped into a domestic format as she leaves one form of authority, her parents, and moves to another equally authoritarian domestic set-up, the marital home. Yet, I think that this is too simplistic an interpretation. A helper does not necessarily mean a subordinate. We assume that and our cultural norms affirm that. Woman and Man are of equal help to one another, otherwise there would have been no reason to create a gender that was wholly different yet still complementary to one another. (I am going to leave the biology stuff outside this discussion and focus purely on the emotional and spiritual needs of a partnership.) Whilst we can have incredible moments of revelation and discovery on our own, most of our pleasant memories involve another person. God thus devised a solution.

Adam's description gives us food for thought. He doesn't rhapsodise woman with a long treatise on the size of her derriere or her perky yet still full bosoms. No, instead he describes her as 'bone of my bones and flesh of my flesh'. She is part of him, not outside of him, not to be objectified or belittled. After all, it is difficult to objectify something that is in essence you. Woman is intrinsically part of man and vice versa. A lot of what creates relationship breakdowns and conflict is when we focus on the differences. In fact there is a library of books based on the premise that we are innately different and never the twain shall meet, that we must struggle through, despite the differences. Yet what if we consider and celebrate the fact that we are innately like each other, if we take time to revere how we are created to keep one another's company, to comfort, to assist. If we think of one another as a protracted reflection of self, that we are as likely to be hurt by the same sort of actions and words, that we need the same sort of affection and assurances, our point of engagement shifts radically and so does the level of reward.

Dating disaster deliverance

So you're on the date. Turned up on time, maybe even chose to splash out on something suitably fabulous and the date is turning out to be more clapped-out motor than sporty Jag. Most of us have been on one of these dates. The conversation is stilted, barely moving out of neutral never mind speeding along in fifth gear.

The vibe between you and date is more noxious fumes than fragrant, and if you were to compare how comfortable you felt perching on that stool or walking along that river bank with him you would more than likely liken it to a lumpy car chair with sticky vinyl head rest than a gloriously squishy tan leather interior which smelt of pure luxury and had deep pile carpeting to press your feet into. There is also a desperation that can creep in on a date, especially if it has been built up either by us or by others. We can feel a pressure to make it work and have a really fantastic time and, if there is no spark, to pour our own version of emotional 'lighter fluid' to create a suitably dynamic experience. However, these incendiary tactics, which vary from more wine (always a *bad* look), to agreeing with everything the other person says (so as to appear to be compatible) often blow up in our faces. We either make a fool of ourselves at best or find ourselves accidentally-on-purpose in a relationship with someone with whom we actually have nothing in common and who we may even find faintly annoying (no one to blame but yourselves, ladies, for meekly saying 'Oh yes, of course, I agree' to everything he said). Yet I implore anyone who reads this to really absorb the truth of God's plan for us:

> … the LORD your God goes with you; he will never leave you nor forsake you.
>
> **Deuteronomy 31:6**

Yes, on that nightmare date God was there with you. He may have even had a chuckle as you attempted to do a come hither stare and ended up looking like someone with a squint (I do have a squint and hence gave up this tactic long ago), or you attempted to impress the dude with your food knowledge and ended up with a big dollop of ketchup on the middle of your cream top! **Deuteronomy** chronologically covers the time of the Israelite Exodus out of Egypt, but there are many parallels in our dating life to the Exodus. It too is a journey and it too can feel extremely lonely and excessively long, especially if your experiences seem to tend more towards the nightmare night rather than the dream date scenario. Also, like in the Exodus, we may be fleeing from our own 'mental captivity' rather than a physical one, where old thoughts or broken relationships have kept us stagnant for too long. But here we see God is with us on that journey and the permanence of his presence is writ large in this verse. He does not ditch *you*, get bored easily or be angry for long. It's difficult to put that kind of belief in another person. It goes back to our own expectations or past again. And whilst yes, outright rejection is horrible, and endless bad date stories can wear down even the hardiest heart, God's love is incorruptible. Not only is it completely selfless but also it never fluctuates. We are all seeking love but it is only in God that we encounter a love that is limitless and a relationship where the fear of rejection is absent and disappointment can never be a permanent feature. It is this truth that we must hold up. That a love that is boundless in its enthusiasm and incorruptibility is ours already. So if you are even reading this whilst on a dodgy date (in the ladies' loo of course, or am I the only woman who carries reading material as well as lipstick in her evening purse?) reapply another layer of lipgloss and a spritz of scent and remember that God is right by your

side and would never leave you out to dicey pasture
for ever.

Jewellery and other valuables

In my quest to become a renaissance woman with a
wide array of accomplishments and enough knowledge to get by in most social settings, I started reading
up about gemmology. So I wasn't married yet, but it
didn't hurt to know about facets, carats or the fact that
there were such things as pink sapphires. Perhaps the
most significant thing that I found out on my whistle-
stop tour of various websites on the internet was that
how a gemstone was set and cut made all the difference. Sometimes it was quite literally all in the setting,
the Cartier engagement ring being a classic example of
this with its pronged setting complete with 'C for
Cartier' shaped joins. My ultimate virtual selection was
an Asscher cut solitaire on a platinum band, as my
hands aren't large enough to take baguette shoulders.
However, as I ogled at sites of names that I could
barely pronounce and with jewels the size of quail eggs
I was reminded of a famous prelude in Proverbs:

> A wife of noble character who can find? She is
> worth far more than rubies.
>
> **Proverbs 31:10**

Returning to the passage in my bible, the words
lingered with me, as there I had been on sites admir-
ing gems of great value and in this famous passage in
Proverbs 31:10–31 a woman's worth was considered
far more than a string of precious stones. Furthermore,
the precious stones that many women, myself included,

hanker after from their intendeds as outward expressions of the love that they share were not even commensurate of the woman's character herself. In the above verse it is quite explicitly posited that the discovery, the journey and the quest for that woman of noble character is Herculean in itself, that it's a 'pop the champagne and let out a sigh of relief' moment for the lucky chap when you do find her. And as for those jewels the eager beaver geezer had saved up for to impress the lady in question? They are nothing if not entirely inconsequential to the woman herself. It is also worth noting that it is her character that really stands out and is of value rather than how she looks. The passage talks at length of the way she works and conducts herself in light of her husband, and appearances really take a back seat in all of this as later on in the passage it is stated:

> *Charm is deceptive, and beauty is fleeting; but a woman who fears the LORD is to be praised.*
> **Proverbs 31:30**

Her relationship with God, her identity within him and her commitment to following his paths, as indicated in the mentioning of her having the fear of the Lord, is what really marks her out for distinction and gets her the beautiful gemstone accolade.

So if the character is of greatest value, the spirit of a woman as it were, the very essence of her, what of the exterior? How do we value those? And how do we figure out who gets to handle said valuables and when? It becomes increasingly tricky to try and separate the body and the spirit, especially as when one is alive our spirit is being housed, albeit temporarily, in our body.

If as indicated in the passage of Proverbs our character and essence are of value it follows that our bodies are also. Which brings us neatly to those other 'valuables' we all possess, that have members of the opposite sex 'oohing' and 'ahhing' in almost the same husky tones as I did on the fine jewellery sites.

Our bodies and the giving of them are of great value. A facile remark perhaps, but an important one to make. One only has to look at the industries built around priming and prepping our bodies for their proverbial close-ups: the beauty parlour, the gym, I could go on but I shan't, to realise the importance society places on being picture perfect for the horizontal lambada with your leading man of choice. What of the context of this activity and the repercussions? Surprisingly, or at least surprisingly for me when I first read it, tucked between the books of Ecclesiastes and Isaiah there are a few saucy passages to be found in the bible. The Song of Songs, or the Song of Solomon as it is sometimes referred to, is a love poem which lengthily tells of a courtship, divided up in such a way that we hear the male and the female's take on their relationship. Why is it in the bible? It is one of the few books in the bible (another being Esther) that does not include or mention God directly. Clerics and scholars have pontificated over its inclusion, divided by whether it is an allegory for the love God has for us, his church. But taking it at its most literal it is a telling template for a sexual relationship that is God-breathed. For a start, the first four books are courtship at its most full-on and romantic; we have the beloved, the female warning us:

> *Daughters of Jerusalem, I charge you by the gazelles and by the does of the field: Do not arouse or awaken love until it so desires.*
>
> **Song of Songs 2:7**

And her lover, in a lengthy soliloquy about her beauty and general all-round wonderfulness, commenting that:

> *You are a garden locked up, my sister, my bride; you are a spring enclosed, a sealed fountain.*
>
> **Song of Songs 4:12**

And once again the bible doesn't disappoint with the gemstone analogies as the girl rhapsodies about her chap in **Song of Songs 5:10–16**.

> *His arms are rods of gold set with chrysolite. His body is like polished ivory decorated with sapphires.*
>
> **Song of Songs 5:14**

But perhaps most significantly she closes with this final flourish:

> *His mouth is sweetness itself; he is altogether lovely. This is my lover, this is my friend, O daughters of Jerusalem.*
>
> **Song of Songs 5:16**

If we start with **Song of Songs 2:7** we see a general warning about pressing on full speed before it's entirely necessary. This is no spoiler remark from someone who is far removed from sexual desire because they've taken a monastic vow, or is happily married and regularly sated thank-you very much, as later verses in the book illustrate. Instead this is an entirely 'I know what it's like, ladies, as I'm so in the fray myself' exclamation. The thing about opening a door is it is so much easier to go through it once it's ajar. She is not saying that going through that door is a non-starter for ever and ever, she is merely warning against a full steam ahead approach, of rousing desires before their time.

And what of the man in the piece? Apart from the 'isn't she fab' testimonial he points out another attribute about her in **Song of Songs 4:12**. The lady he loves is a locked garden and untapped spring. The analogy is pretty obvious. She's a virgin. Although, we shouldn't be disheartened if this is not an actuality for us, as virtuous conduct is of equal value and can gain similar effects. What perhaps is more significant is he's not 'getting in there', sampling the dish and generally tucking in as it were, although he has a fair bash at describing what it must be like as in his mind her 'garden' includes high-value crops such as pomegranates, cinnamon and saffron to name but a few (for the full list check out **Song of Songs 4:1–15**)! His desire does not seem to decrease because he hasn't slept with her, quite the contrary.

Finally when we study her desiring heart's stream of consciousness we see something else. Apart from likening him to every exquisite object, substance and precious metal and gemstone that a girl in the Ancient World could have seen, she describes him as both *her lover and her friend*. The two – friendship and sexual intimacy – are indivisible and in this is the key to the profundity of the couple's affection for one another. The physical is all well and good but is naught without the companionship. It is illustrated, too, when the man describes her as 'my sister, my bride'. In churches we often refer to the men in the church as brothers and the females as sisters as we are all reconciled to God's family through Jesus. By calling her his sister, he is echoing this relationship, which is the primary one before the sexual one.

It's not that sex in itself is bad, Song of Songs lyrically evokes just how amazing it is. Nor is it particularly helpful when we as Christians bang on to each other or to our non-Christian friends about the physical and spiritual perils of random shags. Anyone who has been in a broken sexual relationship can recall just how low they felt in the inevitably messy aftermath. Perhaps more instructive is couples taking time to enjoy one another and praise one another's characteristics as seen in **Proverbs 31**, and when they're done with that the marvelling on the physical side could be done with the Song of Songs template in mind; not making any bones of fancying one another but also being aware of appropriate contexts for physical expression. Finally, we'd be wise to not forget the siblinghood we share as being part of humankind created in God's image and loved by him totally. Not for us to treat one another in a harried and cavalier manner gratifying our sensual senses without any thought for the other person's heart or soul. Then there is remembering that we are meant to be friends first and foremost and with friendship comes trust, encouragement and in certain cases a gentle nudge towards temperance. I am aware that for some my musings, and they are merely my own musings, on the whole sex-before-marriage debate may not be quite frontline enough, but as sex is ultimately a private affair between two parties despite what talk shows, Hollywood movies and others might lead us to believe, questions around it are best solved and explored between those two parties after their own quiet reflection and enquiry to biblical teaching. My final point is just as we wouldn't be careless with a priceless jewellery suite, so we should treat our precious bodies which house our greatest treasures, our souls, and which were bought at the most expensive rate ever, Jesus' blood, with equally deliberate care.

When love goes pear-shaped

'You know that you will always be mine.' I remember so clearly how those words made me feel. I was cold and my hair was askew. Never mind that, I thought to myself. He was beautiful, smelt other-worldly and had a voice that was as smooth as vellum paper. You know, the sort to whom you imagine writing profound, adoring notes of love and leaving them underneath gazillion thread count linen. And as for his arms wrapped around me in a hug, they were a salve in themselves. Those words made me feel safe and secure. It did not matter that my room was not a suite at the Crillon and that much of my life lay uncertain. There was a permanence in the love he was offering. But the human heart is funny and circumstances and choices buffet us all about. And people break up. We did. What added to my whole push-face with God vibe was that he picked someone else. A girl that in my eyes was not offering half as much as me. I mean, she did not know about all his favourite things. She couldn't possibly possess my wit or ability to amass trivia, tunes and shoes with such alacrity. It wasn't fair. I had done the whole courtship in Christ stuff. I had prayed and thanked God about the relationship. Of course I had erred occasionally and my behaviour was not always Christ-gives-you-a-gold-star stuff but surely not so badly as to lose what I thought would always be mine – the love of my life? So, after the requisite Bombay Sapphire gin drinking, floor length silk nightie wearing in the middle of the afternoon and Billie Holliday and Mary J. Blige listening marathon, I consulted the good book. Two things struck me about the quality and character of love described: it was both selfless and endless.

C. S. Lewis, in his excellent book *The Four Loves*, beautifully highlighted the different characters of love. The word for love in Greek appears in many forms; there is the love between friends *Phileo*, the love between lovers *Eros* and then there is the divinely inspired *Agape* love. Agape love is selfless and it is this word that is used when describing the sort of love God has for us.

Paul's passage on love (**1 Corinthians 13**) has been described as the clearest description of divine love.

> *Love is patient, love is kind. It does not envy, it does not boast, it is not proud. It is not rude, it is not self-seeking, it is not easily angered, it keeps no record of wrongs.*

1 Corinthians 13:4–5

There is no tit for tat in Agape. Agape love is about loving whatever the weather, regardless of praise or recognition. And amid its 'steady-on, don't mind meness' lies its potency. How many times do people ever try and give another person this sort of love? Many say the last time they felt loved unconditionally was as a child by parents. And even this unconditional love can become clouded as one grows older and parental expectations get in the way. But do we love our boyfriends and husbands in this kind of way? And how would that Agape love revolutionise the relationship? If you are reading this having already bagged your Brad or Taye substitute then I ask: how much of your love is based on what he has to do? Is expected to do? Has done for you in the past? How much of your love is contingent on nothing else save him being him? Isn't that the sort of love that we would all like? Whilst it is wonderful to be admired and I commend any man who can notice a new dress, haircut and, for extra bonus points, accessory changes, it is ultimately the essence of us that we want to be most appreciated. Often it is fear or the nagging feeling that maybe this is not enough that creates so much of the agony in relationships. Him thinking that he is little more than an additional cash-point so of course he is within with his rights to have some 'outside' fun, and she thinking that the sum total of her worth to him is in her dress size and thus it's perfectly reasonable to start abusing her body in the quest for that.

When love goes awry it is usually to do with the fact that we have taken the Agape element out of it. But when love becomes less about the other person and more about us, then it is little more than self-idolatry. Sometimes this self-idolatry can be inversed as it was in my earlier case. You see, I had taken his flesh-led proclamation of 'always being his girl' (however sweetly it was intended from my intended) and put it up on some sort of pedestal where it was as indefatigable as a promise from God. So when it proved to be an inconstant human emotion I turned the love that I had previously expressed outwardly to my intended, inwardly against myself. I was thinking I was a reject and hence must be viewed by God in a similar light. It is in this place that the negative thought processes flourished in my heart and I grew to dislike myself with the same vigour I felt God disliked me, and with the same blind passion I had loved my intended. None of this was in any way centred on the truths regarding God's love for us and the sort of love he expects us to have for others that are beautifully explored in **1 Corinthians 13**.

The thing about self-pity and overly indulgent remorse at the end of a love affair is it can often be a very prideful emotion. I use the word prideful advisedly:

> *Pride goes before destruction, a haughty spirit before a fall.*
> **Proverbs 16:18**

If we're not careful and we choose to sit in a cesspool of melancholy when our love affairs go wrong we can end up in the same sort of destructive patterns of behaviour that imprison and constrain. A haughty spirit does not necessarily concern itself with thinking how fantastic it is: it can also articulate how terminally useless it is. As we take time to think, discuss internally or externally and seek out real life examples, which we may have to create in actuality so that we have our very own 'live playback', we grow quite 'pleased' with ourselves for knowing the real scoop on who we are and what will 'always happen'. We become the sort of people who make bold affirmations along the lines of 'I know I will never find love again.' Or 'All guys are rubbish anyway and are bound to tin you at the earliest opportunity, or at the very least cheat on you the moment you gain five pounds after the honeymoon.' In short we start blocking our breakthrough and limiting our opportunities. Or our haughty spirit does. Yet we are not omniscient. Indeed, whilst seeking out answers to questions is something we all thrive upon and is central to the human condition, so too is the realisation that we will never be privy to God's intentions for a situation. It is not for us to second guess, and whilst we can learn a great deal from what has happened to us we must always focus on being more than the sum total of our past experiences. We must also seek to truly entertain and embrace the possibility – no, the absolute certainty – of an improved existence because of God's boundless love for us.

WORK

WORK

'So what do you do?'

It's such a frequent question, probably the first one muttered after a basic enquiry of a person's name. For some, answering the question is an opportunity to talk about something that is a source of pride. They are absolutely elated to tell the world that they have it all. That they are working in their dream job or career. That they are recognised as leading lights in their field. And that, yes, it pays so handsomely that three holidays a year and the latest offerings from the luxury car market are not a vague possibility, but a distinct reality due to their tidy remuneration. For others, the question brings with it a twinge of pain. The job they're in might not exactly set them on fire with excitement, but it pays the bills, even though they might have a dormant expectation of something better. For those who are unemployed it might bring with it feelings of social inadequacy, as they are spectators or passengers rather than fully fledged participants in the job economy. Yet work is so much more than how much we earn and jobs are so much more than what people think of them.

> *There are different kinds of working, but the same God works all of them in all men.*
> **1 Corinthians 12:6**

We are all different and whatever our working situation is it is all part of God's creation. Pastry chefs are of equal import to paediatricians. After all someone has to make children's favourite chocolate treats as well as get them better! The key phrase is 'the same God works all of them'. God uses everything for his glory. There is no hierarchy. The phrase might be particularly disheartening to the unemployed, but again the same God is at work in seemingly outward inactivity. For in spite of what might be going on in the external, there is always movement and development when we consider our walk with Christ and there is still endless work that lasts a lifetime to be done in the perfecting of our walk.

In the introduction of this book I wrote at length about my own spasmodic career, with its requisite down-time periods of seeming inactivity. I myself have worked in many industries in a variety of functions, from managerial strategist to invisible numerical filing clerk sitting in a windowless office with only an old CD walkman for company. However, God was never absent. There were times when I felt he was disengaged, that he had placed me in work that I had no desire or passion for, that I was being punished for not being good enough, that my dreams were being moved hopelessly and intentionally out of my reach. Yet, in the less than fantastic roles I have met and connected with a variety of people. Sometimes I have learnt things that have come in handy at a later juncture: how else would a non-driver like myself know that a company called Dana Corp are dab hands at making car chassis? Or even known what a car chassis was? I put this juicy tit-bit to use twice. Once, when I found myself in the company of a captain of the motor industry, who was probably sighing at the prospect of sitting next to a clueless chick who had no idea about what he or his organisation did. The second time was on a hot date, again showing my boy-friendly conversation skills to their best ability. In both instances, I thanked God.

During the aforementioned random job, where I had cold-called car manufacturers all around Europe selling them advertising space, using the pseudonym Mara Bling, I chose to recognise that somewhere in the situation, God was present. Even my pseudonym, which had to tally with my real initials, was God-breathed. I took the first name from the Book of Ruth, where Naomi renames herself Mara, meaning 'bitter' in Hebrew, because of the run of bad luck she has experienced. I myself felt that I was bitter about the kind of work I was doing and I wanted God to know that. I also wanted some sort of biblical reference point to emanate every time I put on my headset. As to my choice of Bling for the surname, let's just say I had high aspirations about the commission cheques! However, it was not for me to know the exact shape and form the blessings I would receive from that job would take. Ultimately we are only called to know and hold true to our hearts that God is working in every situation.

Waiting for the call

It is in these very interim jobs that God often prepares us and confirms to us our Divine Calling. People don't talk about callings in this day and age. It seems somewhat anachronistic at best – think Florence

Nightingale and all the other professional do-gooders of the eighteenth and nineteenth century – and entirely other-worldly at worst. I mean, how often do we hear of someone we know being blinded for a couple of days on their way to an offsite or work trip, getting an actual word from God talking directly into their present career and directing them to their calling? **Acts 9** tells of such a story in the conversion of Paul. It is interesting that the author of much of the New Testament and perhaps the greatest evangelist that ever lived had an interim job persecuting Christians. On one level Paul's interim job and his calling could be viewed as being at odds with one another. Yet viewed as an exposition of God's power it makes for compelling reading. What better way to illustrate the transformative nature of God's love than to have an individual who persecuted Christians becoming the *sine qua non* of evangelists? What's more, because he had been persecuting them for so long, Paul already knew all of the objections people had to the faith as well as an understanding of the methodology of persecution and the mind-set of said persecutors. In fact, throughout the Pauline epistles of the New Testament there is evidence both in his style of evangelism and in his story (he was martyred and his last letter, **Philippians**, makes for particularly poignant reading) of his previous role working in tandem with his present one.

A calling does not need to arrive in such a dramatic fashion, but we each have one. Something that has been uniquely placed in us to share, impart, solve or create. It starts with the things that we are good at or enjoy doing anyway and develops still further into us diligently pursuing this activity. Through disciplined application we refine and develop our skills and we earnestly seek opportunities to put our talents into practice.

> *Whatever you do, work at it with all your heart, as working for the Lord, not for men, since you know that you will receive an inheritance from the Lord as a reward. It is the Lord Christ you are serving.*
> **Colossians 3:23–24**

Apart from the fact that callings are God-given, the only other quality they all share is the dedication required on our part to follow them. God calls us to a certain level of activity in an area because of two things. First, God gives us the desires of our hearts and wants us to be in areas where we can flourish, and second because our callings are opportunities for further witness of God's glory. A calling is not just an opportunity to work, pay off the mortgage, have a couple of evenings out a month and maybe a chic city weekend break, although it can provide for all of these things. A calling is to fulfil a particular purpose in God's divine plan. It is about being part of a bigger canvas.

The verses above, taken from Colossians, bring us back to the focus and attitude that we are all meant to have when we are engaged in this kind of work. It's not about skiving off and seeing how little actual work we can do. God is not like a mortal boss who might fail to notice when we slope off early to lunch. He sees it all. Furthermore, the 'salary' that we receive from our calling stretches beyond the earthly realm. It is described in the verse as an 'inheritance' that we will receive as a 'reward'. The word inheritance invokes images of a longstanding relationship, of a bequest that can be passed down the generations, and the word reward conjures up notions of recognition and celebration for our contribution. A calling provides all of these things. Working within our calling does not end with us. It is witness and an example that others will see. Furthermore, God rewards us because he recognises our efforts and wants to celebrate them precisely for the reason that they are a manifestation of his good and glorious creation. Just thinking like that immediately makes a two hours' commute on a wet Monday morning somehow appealing!

There is no such thing as no day off

It might seem contradictory to talk of rest, when we have gone on at length about discipline, callings and jumping out of bed on a Monday morning raring to go, but resting is also an edict from God. It is only in the pausing and reviewing stage that we can get any sense of perspective. In fact, in having that proverbial day off we are following an essential divine precedent:

> By the seventh day God had finished the work he had been doing; so on the seventh day he rested from all his work.

Genesis 2:2

Yes, having done the particularly spectacular task of creating the whole universe, eco-system and all the stuff in between, as well as planning the good purposes that he had for every single human person who has walked, is walking and will walk this earth, God took a day off.

Why? God is after all omnipotent and omniscient, and could in theory keep on going without a cat-nap.

The clues are there earlier in other parts of the creation story. At the end of each creative exertion verses end with an expression of God's pleasure at his handiwork. In fact one phrase gets repeated five times in the first chapter of Genesis:

> ... *God saw that it was good.*
> **Genesis 1:10, 12, 18, 21, 25**

With a final superlative statement:

> *God saw all that he had made, and it was very good.*
> **Genesis 1:31**

In pausing at each juncture of creation and acknowledging the magnificence of his creation, God was placing a value on those efforts. The pause and the acknowledgement can be seen as appreciation and thanksgiving of what had come before and been achieved. It isn't in any way a case of our Lord and Saviour sloping off, as after each day of activity he is off doing more essential works on the universe and other universes around us. There is a valuable message in this pause and value system that God follows. He teaches us that his creation, made in his image, is a model of working that we often forget. We should always try to pause at the end of each task, even if it's internally, to acknowledge the goodness that has come out of it and the pleasure that it will create. Whether it means that our diligent input will result in someone winning a law case, living long enough to see their child's wedding or feeling confident enough to wear a bikini on holiday, it is all good because it is done with a positive intention and result in mind and as such it should be appreciated.

The trap that we often fall into is looking beyond the task in hand. This is not bad in itself, but can often result in our missing out on the triumphs of today and fully celebrating them. A loss of perspective, of viewing and delighting in that moment of 'Wow I really have done a lot of excellent and valuable work' can provide a place for the twin plagues of self-doubt and frustration to take root. 'It was not good enough' we say to ourselves, not because this is necessarily the case but because we failed to pause and appreciate what we had done. 'I'm still behind, I must therefore be useless.' Yes, lagging behind in a task is never ideal, but how about looking at it from the point of what we have done thus far and what we have yet to complete? That way, we are not in a position of defeat but of imminent victory. And as to the old chestnut of work being of such paramount importance and dominance that we do not have the time to spend with family and friends or suffer from constant full-on fatigue and hence don't ever fully engage with them: we must remember that our work and calling are essential to God's plan for us but so too are the people with whom we are called into communion. Extended periods of isolation are often a breeding ground for a morose mind-set. After all, it is with almost regular metronome-like frequency that we will have that wobbly moment when a call, text or email from a loved one can be all the encouragement that we require. If absorbing this truth makes us feel uncomfortable, perhaps it is because we have gotten used to a stress-filled working style as a necessary feature of life. If we are only able to show that we are really working and truly useful in our roles if all other areas of our life take a back seat, then we become indentured servants to our job titles. Worse yet, we have made work into an idol if we give everything of ourselves to it to the detriment of other areas of our lives.

It is easy to succumb to this attitude, even if we are not doing a job that is our calling. For in those instances work is to be endured rather than enjoyed, and so resting is not part of the equation. This mistaken approach not only leads to being ineffective, as we plod along exhausted, but also we miss the point and purpose that God has for us. It is often in the resting times that we are made aware of where God wants us to go next. Whether it's the best strategy to get the most out of your interim job and move towards your divine calling or how to best maximise your calling and reach the most people with it. If we don't choose to pause and rest, to incorporate quiet time, we will never get the chance to experience the fullness of his peace and pin-pricks of his imagination:

> 'For I know the plans I have for you,' declares the LORD, 'plans to prosper you and not to harm you, plans to give you hope and a future.'
> **Jeremiah 29:11**

Learning to accept God's ultimate control over our working lives does not mean that we are slacking off or that we have no idea of where we are going. On the contrary, the above verse illustrates how his plans not only include our prosperity but also that we have a future filled with promise. Confident in this knowledge and knowing that we are in the hands of a benevolent creator we should attempt to bask in his acceptance, be refreshed by his love and be directed by his superior management skills.

The heavenly employment review

There was one company that operated on a 360° assessment of the workers. The concept was thus: you wrote how well you thought you had done in the last quarter and then all of your co-workers wrote what they thought of the work that you had done and finally your boss wrote their thoughts. Then at a pre-determined time you were called into a light airy space (I worked in a very trendy office so dark walnut tables or claustrophobic cubicles were not an option) to discuss what had been written about you and to decide upon 'best ways forward'. I came to learn that old-timers at the company started the campaign for the 360° assessment process long before it was due. The trick was to get as many colleagues on side so that your review would read like the model employee. No matter if you occasionally sloped off early or palmed off your mistakes on subordinates, if in the eyes of the mass you were 'doing good' then all was well. Appearances really were everything.

In contrast, when we look at the work that we do in our lives and how God assesses it at our life's close we see a different model of assessment. The parables that most vividly illustrate the heavenly employment review are the Parable of the Talents (**Matthew 25:14–30**) and the Parable of the Ten Minas (**Luke 19:11–27**). In both we see a master (Jesus) going away (ascending to heaven) and leaving his servants (us lot) in charge of his money (God's creation). Three servants, reflect the differing attitudes we have to the work God has entrusted us with. The first servant takes the opportunity of the responsibility to show his master just how well he can work, in both he gets the best review:

> *'Well done good and faithful servant! You have been faithful with a few things; I will put you in charge of many things. Come and share your master's happiness!'*
> **Matthew 25:21** (see **Luke19:17** for the corollary reward)

The second who works, but not quite to the same degree, perhaps because some days he's inspired and others he doesn't give it 100%, or gets distracted or browses on the net, also gets a reward that's in proportion to his efforts, which though good is not as excellent as the first.

> *'The second came and said, "Sir, your mina has earned five more." His master answered, "You take charge of five cities."'*
> **Luke19:18–19** (see **Matthew 25:22–23**)

The final worker doesn't do anything. He is given the opportunity, sees the others working but rather than redouble his efforts, decides what sort of master he has, the kind of review he's due for and as a result sees no point in putting in any sort of effort. His attitude is reflected in his justification that acts as a prelude before he shows the master the full extent of his lack of work: 'I knew you were a hard man', states

Matthew 25:24. 'I was afraid of you, *because* [my emphasis] you are a hard man', adds **Luke 19:21**, before going on to show the full extent of his lack-adaisical attitude. His punishment is total. Not only does the master rebuke him for having the audacity to second guess what kind of boss he was and what reward he was due for, he also describes the third worker's attitude as 'wicked'. Not only does the third worker fail to share in 'his master's happiness' or enter God's kingdom, but he is thrown 'into darkness' and killed, an allegory for the eternal death one experiences in the darkness of hell.

The parable's closing tableaux are worse than any anonymous envelope with a severance pay cheque and a security guard watching you clear your desk scenario that we experience in our earthly lives, but if we delve deeper we see why the rewards and the penalties are on a much more magnified scale in the heavenly realm. When God gives you a talent or asks you to steward over something that is ultimately his, he is placing you in a senior management role in his company which is a company that if it had a name would probably be called 'All Creation Incorporated' or better yet 'All Creation Unlimited'. This is not an organisation that is affected by stock market wobbles, but its work, as the name of the organisation implies, affects everyone and everything. If the work is left undone or is sloppily executed, there are universal implications. It is for this reason that those who do work diligently get the opportunity to share in God's happiness. It could be that your work as an architect means that someone works or lives in a restful environment, or due to your efforts as an economist, strategies are created that enable people in poor countries to have opportunities to enrich themselves. The joy we experience when we hear of people benefiting from our efforts is heartening and it is often something we often go on to share with those closest to us, so it is perhaps not surprising that God calls us to share in his happiness and the stewardship of the heavenly realm.

And for those aiming for a bonus

If the thought of being a star performer in God's employ hasn't overwhelmed you and you don't think that the fate of the last worker in the above-mentioned parables could ever be you, then one can always go for the next level. There are some people who through no real fault or major efforts of their own have an abundance of talent. We have all met girls like that. A head for facts and figures, beauty-pageant pretty, brilliant at sports, amazing aesthetic sensibilities and always at the forefront of charitable initiatives. In fact if the woman in question wasn't also such a 'nice girl' you'd scream out of a window or throw up into the nearest bucket. However, if that woman is you then here is a further biblical challenge:

> '... From everyone who has been given much, much will be demanded; and from the one who has been entrusted with much, much more will be asked.'
> **Luke 12:48**

Part of a longer passage on watchfulness (see **Luke 12:35–48**), Jesus illustrates how, if you are one of those individuals who is an excelling servant there will be further responsibilities and expectations due to your abilities. Rather like the finance professionals in the City or Wall Street, who have bonuses with a mind-boggling number of zeros at the end, due to the levels of money that they have successfully managed over a set period of time, God expects and demands similar levels of commitment and performance from his elite workers. So the next time you envy the friend who's 'got it all' know too that she is called to work equally hard at all of those talents so that she realises the God-filled potential in *all* of them. And if you're said girl, all I can say is good luck and know that he is with you.

FRIENDSHIPS

Friends are family

Writing about friendships has been tricky and loaded. Why? Because the word seems so thin, too weak to truly reflect the depth of feelings, the levels of trust and exactly how much is at stake with friendships. The old adage often sticks: 'We can choose our friends but we can't choose our family.' Our friends are a reflection of who we are, what we're interested in and where we wish to go. They are separate from what goes on or went on in the home. However, there is a closer synergy between the two: your great aunt who has the love affair with lavender-scented everything and your closest chum are of equal value. After all there are times when we require different sorts of emotional needs to be met. Putting a value judgement on problem-solving, rooting out a bargain, or making us laugh is pointless, as all those actions come from the very same God-made place of love that we all have residing within us. Both family and friend offer us the same security:

> *A friend loves at all times, and a brother is born for adversity.*
> **Proverbs 17:17**

There is a consistency in affection required in our friendships. Taken from the Book of Proverbs this is more than a cosy epithet or empty platitude. In loving us at all times our friends are there as witnesses to our circumstances. It is not for our friends to tire of our woes or in their frustration with our behaviour to withdraw their affection. Our friends love us 'in all times'. Similarly, a brother is born for adversity. Families often come into their own in times of trouble. There is something of the miraculous during periods of crisis management in the acceptance we receive from people who have loved us all our lives. Sometimes a quick word from someone who loves us is all we need by way of encouragement to go the extra mile and overcome. It might be for this reason that friends and family are mentioned together in this same verse. In both relationships we are called to trust, share and encourage, but there are also challenges in being friends in spite and throughout everything.

Whilst very few of us are fortunate enough to come from a *Waltons* or *Cosby Show* family set-up, not all families are a living nightmare, and in the cases where they are they need to be restored to the edifying inter-actions God intended them to be. Our friends and family are both relational set-ups, and their health has a direct relation to how we in turn feel. At the centre of both interactions are friendships. Whilst this might seem strange – after all how can one's mother be one's buddy? – it is not too 'out there', as, in a Christian con-text, we are all siblings in Christ, struggling with the various shortcomings of our humanity, and thus all equal. Our interaction with all of those closest to us involves us being friends with them as they affirm and accept us and we reciprocate.

Green-eyed monsters and other gremlins

Probably the greatest blocks in female friendships, whether they are between contemporaries, siblings or mothers and daughters, are envy and condemnation. The last of the Ten Commandments is worth considering at this point:

> 'You shall not covet your neighbour's house ... or anything that belongs to your neighbour.'
> **Exodus 20:17**

This commandment doesn't often get much of a look-in and people shy away from the severity of it, and yet it is covetousness and envy that cause the most damage between friends. We have all at one point or another been afflicted by the particularly unpleasant and more than a shade embarrassing and icky pang that comes when we're envious. It might be something minor, like our friend's effortlessly pulled-together look, or her ability to befriend new people. Some of us might be envious of a friend whose career is in orbit whilst ours languishes in the boonies, still others are tormented by a friend's physical beauty, desperately wishing to own the perfect pins, cup-runneth-over bosoms and glossy hair ourselves. However, it is testament to the poisonous power of covetousness that it made it into the Ten Commandments.

One story remains with me. A girl of especially heart-stopping beauty complained bitterly of her lack of friends. Yet many of the women around her assumed that she was conceited, and when questioned further admitted they were envious of her ability to draw men to her effortlessly. The scenario was confounded by her mother, who saw in her daughter's bloom the passing away of her own youth and desirability and accorded her daughter an appropriately frosty interaction. The mother's justification? 'When people stop, it's not to look at me, but to admire her. I'm rendered invisible.' The sentence is all the more heartbreaking as the girl, clearly her mother's 'mini-me', had now lost the one person with whom she could have shared her problem of loneliness and isolation due to others' envy of her extreme beauty.

Envy within friendships, left unchecked, spreads into the heart of the relationship. Instead of offering loving connection, we turn our companions' situations and attributes into internal adversaries. Their triumphs are no longer opportunities for collective celebration, but a reminder of our own failures. Their abilities are no longer gifts that can be shared but highlighters of our own inadequacies. Neither is the pain one-way. As we withdraw, lost and sick in our own covetous, envy-filled emotional hole, our friend is left lonely and unhappy, unable to share, be comforted and encouraged. To progress in our friendships we must uphold the primacy of love and ask God to root out the negative emotions that attempt to bind. We must also focus on the incredible giftings that are uniquely placed in ourselves and the contribution that we make, that is nothing to do with our friends and more likely everything to do with why they love and support us so much.

The other monster that often blurs our friendships is condemnation. It is easy to list the flaws we see in our own friends and family. It is easy, too, to judge their contribution to the relationship, see them lacking and wanting and deem them unworthy. However, there are many examples where God expects a different response from us:

> *'Why do you look at the speck of sawdust in your brother's eye and pay no attention to the plank in your own eye?'*
> **Matthew 7:3**

When we judge our friends rather than help them, we attempt to 'play God', which is intrinsically wrong as we too are riddled with our own flaws. It is so easy to focus on others' faults, especially the faults of those whom we are closest to – after all, we have had plenty of time to observe them and get wound up. Those who know me know that I rarely get anywhere close to on time (I blame my two days extra stay in the womb as the beginnings of a very bad habit). Over the years I have attempted to improve upon my tardiness, but for it to be used as evidence of me being an uncaring friend would be unfair just as it would be unreasonable for me to pick an irritating trait as a reason to abandon a friend. We need to ask, 'What are the benefits of keeping a tally of all the wrongs we have suffered at the hands of one another?' Would we like it, if we felt our character was on permanent trial with those closest to us? Would we not all concede that our relationships would suffer in authenticity as the strains of 'being perfect' all of the time began to take their toll? Often, focusing on others' flaws gives us the perfect get-out clause to not concentrate on our own areas for improvement. Some of us gain our self-esteem from measuring ourselves against others, and congratulating ourselves silently or otherwise for not being such a consummate basket-case. But it is a lonely place, residing in our own elevated place of pride. We all know that we aren't perfect and yet, as we distance ourselves from our friends and family, the relationships which would best be equipped to help us improve our potential lie untended.

Intimacy-phobes

There are some who collect art, others, slightly poorer, who go for accessories and then there are those who collect acquaintances. Seeking out connection with new people is no bad thing in itself. I myself am a notorious 'hopper' at parties. Flitting from clusters of people, snatching jokes, anecdotes and dances with boundless enthusiasm. It is part of the rich tapestry of my life that I have been fortunate enough to be exposed to so many different sorts of people. However, professional acquaintance collectors, as I call them, are those people who are unable to let their guard down long enough to allow true friendship to grow. To be a friend is risky. There are no guarantees or a prescribed framework that the friendship will follow. As in affairs of the heart, we may end up hurt.

I fell out with one friend on a major scale. Our friendship would best be described as tempestuous but we had doggedly stayed in one another's lives. After our final falling out, which sadly was over every-thing and nothing in particular, I paused to pray and analyse what had gone wrong. The overriding sense I received in these quiet times was that there had been a lack of intimacy in our relationship. My friend had never trusted me enough. Our friendship was doomed to only go so far from the outset. Without the trust, acceptance and celebration of one another we were lost. Furthermore, without intimacy we were doomed to skate over the surfaces of one another's lives. In times of adversity I was furious for my friend's absence or seeming ambivalence. However, it was equally unrealistic for me to expect anything from someone who had never let their guard down towards me. Put simply, our friendship, though long in length had never grown in depth.

> If one falls down, his friend can help him up.
> But pity the man who falls and has no-one to help
> him up!
> **Ecclesiastes 4:10**

The loss of intimacy in a friendship is the loss of an opportunity to experience true companionship. It is only when we allow ourselves to be exposed for our friends to see the tender wounds of our heart that they can reach out and place a soothing balm on them. Our friends, as the author of Ecclesiastes writes, can help us up when we fall down. To those who reject the opportunity to let their guard down and go beyond the cocktail party chatter there lies a pitiful and ultimately lonely existence. The choice, as with everything, is in our hands but the benefits, when placed next to the alternatives, far outweigh the perceived risks.

Chums' crash-course

Like all the other areas of our lives we have explored so far, there is a convenient biblical model of how to 'do friendships'. Perhaps the most intimate title Jesus gave himself was that of friend. In the bible he is described as 'Son of Man', which may be difficult to fathom and truly understand for those of us who've never absorbed ourselves in Christology. Then there is 'Son of God', a term we may feel makes him far removed from our problems, as he is the child of the all-knowing creator. We also have Jesus described as 'rabbi' or 'teacher', which may give the impression of him, chalk-in-hand, ready to give us all a double detention or send us to the headmaster's office for morally slipping up. By also being our friend, Jesus is showing us that he understands us, the world we live in and the concerns of our heart. What's more, like the true friend he is, he wants us to share our burdens with him that we might be lifted up by him.

When we examine the kind of friend Jesus was, we see the true extent of going the extra mile and self-sacrifice that is witnessed in true friendships:

> *'Greater love has no-one than this, that he lay down his life for his friends.'*
> **John 15:13**

Jesus loved his friends so much that he died for them. The verse above, spoken the night before he died on the cross, shows the true extent of his affection. Whilst no one would advocate that we must die for our loved ones to prove our love, this verse is nevertheless extremely instructive. Laying down one's life could also be understood as putting down our own personal concerns. Not thinking about ourselves and our own selfish needs. Truly being engaged *and* present for our friends. When we lay down our lives and with them our concerns, we open up fully to our friends' needs, and it is only then that we are able to fully meet them.

Almost as important as putting to one side our own self-interest in our relations with our loved ones, is being demonstrative. For those of us who grew up in undemonstrative families this can be tricky at best. Again we can take our cue from Jesus who:

> 'Having loved his own who were in the world, he now showed them the full extent of his love.'
>
> **John 13:1**

This preamble comes at the beginning of the passage that describes Jesus washing his disciples' feet (the whole story can be found in **John 13:1–7**). It's interesting that before we get to the feet-washing part of the story, we have this verse setting the scene: Jesus had already loved his friends in the world and yet that alone didn't quite cut it. He was now seeking an opportunity to illustrate and demonstrate the full extent of his love. We have all had moments when words did not suffice and we needed to actually *do something* to show just how much we cared. It is often these acts that remain imprinted on our minds. There is the friend who opens up their home in times of crisis; the friend who will take you out for a full-on session of dining, dancing and general merry-making to cheer you up. The friend who collects you from the airport, drives you home and has not only tidied your home, done all your laundry and sorted through your post, but also packed your larder and fridge with the choicest edible goodies from Fortnum and Mason. Okay, the last one isn't a friend but an angel, but you get the picture! It is when we have these tangible examples of their love that we are reassured as well as inspired and emboldened to reciprocate.

When Jesus bathed the disciples' feet he did something quite extraordinary. He abased himself for their benefit, breaking away from cultural and customary norms and expectations to show them what they meant to him as friends. Their initial resistance did not deter him and we are called to mimic this too when our own friends become distant, confused or uncomfortable when we reach out to them in a way that they have never seen or experienced before. To be the friend we all want and desperately need, we couldn't do much better than to follow Jesus' model:

> *'I have set you an example that you should do as I have done for you.'*
> **John 13:15**

In washing the disciples' feet Jesus was doing so much more than giving his friends a version excursion of a divine pedicure. He was also showing how at times we might have to take on a role of extreme humility in the friendship. By being the humble party in a situation, we are, like Jesus, generously showering our friends with acts of kindness and generosity. Conversely, there are also seasons when we are called to receive graciously and not ask questions about the whys and the wherefores like the disciples do. It's so terribly English to say something along the lines of 'Oh no, you really shouldn't have' when we are faced with incredible giving, when in fact all we need to do is receive the gift of friendship, be thankful for it, reflect on the quality of what we have and pass on to others what has been graciously given to us.

THE
NEXT STEP

This devotional was meant to be an invitation to explore perennial themes that occupied the women around me. There was no particular game-plan; indeed the writing of the devotional came about entirely by accident (complete with generous loaning of computers from a wide array of people) although I like to view it as divine providence.

The biblical expositions are by no means comprehensive or conclusive and I would encourage people to read the various passages I have highlighted in full for themselves, as in a book of this size there is only really room for bite-sized insights. Call it canapé-Christianity, rather than full-on in-depth analysis. When I decided upon the title of this book, *Heaven in your Handbag*, I wanted to encapsulate the omnipresence of God in every woman's life. Just as we would never leave the house without a handbag of some description, so God always travels with us. In our dreams, or for those with especially fortunate realities, we might rock a Fendi Spy one day, a Chloë Paddington the next, and a Chanel tote to Sunday service. However, God is able to meet all our requirements and respond to all of our needs, and the fantastic news is his word matches our every mood and state and is infinitely more heavenly than the wish list of bags, food and other luxury goods that I have mentioned throughout this book.

Finally, I wanted to write a devotional that was small enough to fit into a handbag, so that women could travel with the book and be reminded that God loves us all and wants to be part of our lives. I have no idea how well this will be received or exactly what God wants me to do next but I always take the following words from Hebrews as encouragement:

> ... let us throw off everything that hinders and the sin that so easily entangles, and let us run with perseverance the race marked out for us.
>
> **Hebrews 12:1**

If I use the race analogy as a starting point for describing my journey, I would say I was exhausted when I started writing this, as I know many of you may be right now. As time progressed I fell into various emotional cramps and stitches, convinced that I was mistaken and this was an entirely self-indulgent exercise, but as I sprinted towards the end of this project I began to realise that this was entirely for God's glory and was merely my small contribution to his creation, or Kingdom, around me. It's my hope and prayer that this book will be the start of an amazing race that each woman who reads it will run. Or that it touches those who have already embarked on their race to move more energetically. It's not a competition, as each of us has a different course and all of us have been especially equipped to run on our particular terrain. In the journey that we take we will discover our selves and start to see those around us in an entirely different light, and as we draw nearer to God our all-loving creator, friend and counsellor we will learn to persevere, to triumph and ultimately to enjoy every divinely authored step we take.

Cheeky seconds

Family and friends know that I love nothing more than second helpings whether it's apple crumble and custard or another plate of grilled meat. After all, if the dish is delicious and there's plenty to go round for everyone, why not? So in the same spirit I felt there were still a few extra God-inspired morsels that I could fit into this devotional even though the previous paragraph was its original close.

First of all a brief epilogue. Since finding a publisher (my thanks to all the team at Darton, Longman and Todd, especially Brendan Walsh), I went home to Uganda for an extended period of time. Again, not planned, just as this book was not. When I got there I was given the opportunity to see how amazing God is and how accents and cultural reference points might change but the young Christo chicks about town faced many of the same challenges as my friends in the west. Why do I include this? Not to be trite, but just because it is so easy to think that you're the only person with a particular problem or going through an issue, but there are so many others in countries far away that are facing similar trials. Not only, but also, it is in the sharing of stories, the praying, laughing and crying together that the healing begins in earnest. I was also inspired and encouraged by people's responses in Uganda to the notion of the devotional. It is so easy when one lives in a predominantly secular society as the west has become, to think you are well and truly 'out there' in writing a genre of book that was last heavily in vogue a few centuries ago when one child taking holy orders was common in many families, and walking around with your nose in a bible was not enough to get the person sitting next to you on a train to move a couple of seats.

To assist in the widening of this community of modern Christo chicks about town, the original email ministry also continues although now it's been up-graded to a website (www.heaveninyourhandbag.com) with biblical expositions and shared testimonies as well as the chick chit-chat that I for one love indulging in! Finally I was also struck by the fact that many of my readers may not be 'churched', but after reading this book might be thinking that now is as good a time as any to purchase a bible for study and reflection. The other 'good news', bibles come in super-small sizes so no need for a triceps workout when moving around with one. There are a number of different translations, so you can shop around for the one that suits you best. And for the most style conscious of us, Smythson, the luxury stationers, have yummy pink hardback leather bound King James editions that look as good decorat-ing the coffee table as anything else and are miles more relevant.

I have also included a brief verse-to-fit-the-mood glossary. Obviously, there are many more than are listed below, but in the spirit of running that race I invite you all to enjoy exploring the word that never goes out of fashion.

As for my own personal four-faceted journey here's the update: I like myself a whole lot more than I did at the beginning of this process. I am learning to enjoy every step of it and not to be stressed out about not being privy to all the minutiae of my future existence. God has it all in hand and as long as I keep on the 'well done good and faithful servant' path, and that Jesus says it to me some day at the beginning of my eternal future, all will be well.

Peace and blessings,

Mazzi xx

A BIBLICAL BABE'S
GUIDE TO
THE GOOD BOOK

First some useful factoids. There are sixty-six books in the bible, thirty-nine in the Old Testament and twenty-seven in the New Testament. There are 1189 chapters and 31,173 verses. The chapter in the middle of the bible is Psalm 117, the longest chapter is Psalm 119, the shortest chapter is Psalm 117 and the shortest verses are John 11:35 and Thessalonians 5:17. Why the nerdy factoids? Because I love amassing random knowledge and I figured starting with the obvious is as good a warm-up as any!

If you are tackling the bible for the first time I would recommend starting with the gospels (**Matthew**, **Mark**, **Luke** and **John**) first. In them you will find the story of Jesus, his ministry, his death and his resurrection. All of the parables are also in the gospels and so are the miracles, which for those who aren't at church on a regular basis are still familiar enough. For the literature buffs amongst us you will probably also discover turns of phrase or verses that have found a way into the classics such as Shakespeare, Hardy and the like, and for those who like their fine art some of the most famous renaissance paintings such as *The Transfiguration* by Raphael and *The Annunciation* by Da Vinci depict famous passages in the gospels.

Once you've explored the gospels, the Pauline

epistles give an overview of many common church teachings and the Book of Acts gives a history of the early church and evangelising process as well as introducing the Holy Spirit and the role it plays in a believer's life today. For the novice bible babe I would suggest reading just a small portion at a time, as rather like dark chocolate tart it can sometimes be both very rich and hard to digest all in one go.

With the Old Testament, the books tend to be longer and the stories don't always follow a neat chronological sequence, however the obvious ones such as **Genesis**, **Exodus**, **1 Samuel** and **2 Samuel** also feature enough familiar characters (Adam, Eve, Moses and the Ten Commandments, Joseph and his coat of many colours, Noah and the Ark, David and Goliath) and again, even if you never read these stories in Sunday school, you've probably watched the movie, heard the musical and seen someone wearing the t-shirt. Of course the Old Testament book that makes an appearance in hotel bedside tables everywhere is **Psalms** as it's often teamed up with the New Testament. **Psalm 23** is a one-size-fits-all winner, but I'd also recommend **Psalm 91** for when you or those around you are in grave or mortal danger, **Psalm 139** when you need a reminder of just how well God knows you and cares, and **Psalm 46** when your back is against the wall.

Tricky, but extremely rewarding, are the so-called 'prophetic books' – **Isaiah, Jeremiah, Lamentations, Ezekiel** and **Daniel** – which cover the prelude to and the fall of Jerusalem as well as the deportation to Babylon. In these books one starts to see a pattern of people's rebellion against God and how it inevitably leads to disastrous consequences. We also see prophecies that are realised in the New Testament in these books, as well as in the 'twelve minor prophets', which run from **Hosea** to **Malachi**. A good study bible is a must here, as it will give you the corollary texts so that you can read and review between the two testaments. The prophetic books are also an increasingly popular hunting ground for original baby's names amongst my Christo mates. I know of several adorable-looking Malachis, Amoses and Joels although I have yet to meet a baby Habakkuk. Perhaps it's just a case of one plosive syllable too many or not having a cutesy enough shortening.

If you're looking for some positive female role models who are not just in the background or the wives of someone a lot more famous, a good place to start is the Old Testament, where we have two books devoted entirely to women and another where a woman is one of the individuals who gets her own mention. First there is Deborah who appears in **Judges 4–5**. A prophetess by training, Deborah is recorded as leading Israel. She was not merely a figurehead, she led the Israelites in battle and was a political strategist, and under her rule we are told that Israel had peace for forty years. Not bad work for a girl indeed! Second there is **Ruth**; all the elements for a good chick read are there. Early widowhood, a beautiful refugee living with her bitter mother-in-law and forced to take a rubbish job in a rich man's field to make ends meet. Except of course, due to her faithfulness (she followed God rather than return home to a polytheist society) and her conscientious work ethic (picking ears of corn in the midday sun – not exactly the ideal temp job), she catches the eye of the rich field owner (Boaz) who after a quick flirtation on the threshing floor egged on by her mother-in-law (you have to read it to get it) she ends up marrying him, pushing out baby Obed, starting the lineage of David and thus Jesus! If that's not really your bag and you prefer your women in all their regal splendour saving the day, rather than as significant matriarchs, then the book of **Esther** is the book for you. Again we have a woman with a heart first and foremost for God, who thanks to her position in the palace uncovers a plot to kill all the Jews. She does a total three-day fast and in this humbled mind state presents the case of the Jews before her husband who just so happens to be the king. In short it could be seen as the ultimate PowerPoint presentation as the future of a whole people lay in her hands. She achieved it and secured her people's safety.

For those quick fixes, the 'I've only got two minutes before I face folk' situations, listed below are some short verses. These are by no means conclusive but they're a start, which with further reading one can easily add to.

So, ladies:

- *If you feel tired*: Try **Matthew 11:28–30**. Short, sweet and, because it is Jesus himself speaking, entirely on point.
- *If it's decision time*: **Jeremiah 17:7–10**. I have personally used this one and I cannot get enough of it!
- *If you're so downtrodden you've gone right through the pavement/sidewalk*: **Lamentations 3:21–27**.